Schools Council Art and Craf
8 to 13 Project

USING CONSTRUCTIONAL MATERIALS

Schools Council
Art and Craft Education 8–13 Project

The project was set up to investigate art education and curriculum development for the 8–13 age group. It set out to make known and co-ordinate advances in art and craft teaching, bridging the gap particularly between primary and secondary schools, and to re-examine the contribution which art and the crafts, as an autonomous study, can make to children's development and how they can assist in the establishment of a flexible school curriculum. The main objective of the project team was to determine the nature of children's creative experience and to reach a finer understanding of the conditions which encourage their creative and imaginative growth.

MATERIALS PRODUCED
HANDBOOK
Children's Growth through Creative Experience
Art and Craft Education 8–13
This handbook is intended not only for teachers but for all those concerned with the education of children within the age-range of 8–13. It includes the findings of the Research Officers' detailed observation of children and teachers in schools, and of the conditions which favour or hinder creative work.
SOURCEBOOKS
Using Natural Materials by Seonaid Robertson
Using Constructional Materials by Michael Laxton
Using Objects by Renée Marcousé

Three supporting booklets which explore in depth suggestions and ideas for teachers in relation to the three sources, which are indicated in their titles.
DISCUSSION MATERIALS
These eleven sets of discussion material are in the form of half-frame film-strips with taped commentary. These are for use by groups of teachers in Teachers' Centres, in Colleges of Education, or elsewhere.

This discussion material is not intended to direct teachers or students to any pre-determined line of development in their work, but to promote debate on the values and purposes behind art and craft education.

THE TITLES	AREA OF WORK
Metropolis	Construction
Imagining with Clay	Clay work
Personal Adornment	Craft
Art in Transfer	Study of art/craft work
From Pleasure They Create	Museum studies
Messing about or Achieving Control?	Painting
Resistant Materials	Craft
What Have We Learnt?	Construction
Fantasy	Construction
Waste Materials	2- and 3-dimensional work
Whose Objectives?	Painting

Schools Council Art and Craft Education
8 to 13 Project

Michael Laxton

USING CONSTRUCTIONAL MATERIALS

VAN NOSTRAND REINHOLD COMPANY
New York · Cincinnati · London · Toronto · Melbourne

Van Nostrand Reinhold Company Regional Offices:
New York Cincinnati Chicago Millbrae Dallas

Van Nostrand Reinhold Company International Offices:
London Toronto Melbourne

Copyright © Schools Council Publications 1974

Library of Congress Catalog Card Number 73 14360
ISBN 0-442-29999-0

Printed in Great Britain by Jolly and Barber Ltd., Rugby.

Published by Van Nostrand Reinhold Company, 450 West
33rd St., New York, N.Y. 10001, and Van Nostrand
Reinhold Company Ltd., 25–28 Buckingham Gate,
London SW1E 6LQ.

16   15   14   13   12   11   10   9   8   7   6   5   4   3   2   1

Library of Congress Cataloging in Publication Data

Laxton, Mike.
Using constructional materials.

1. Handicraft – Study and teaching.   I. Title.
TT168.L34   745.5'07   73-14360
ISBN 0-442-29999-0

Contents

Chapter 1   Our Responsibilities   7

Chapter 2   Children, Materials and Tools   18

Chapter 3   Problems and Possibilities   27

Chapter 4   Construction and Processes of
             Fabrication   43

Chapter 5   Starting Points   58

Chapter 6   Facilities   78

             Index   84

Chapter 1

Our Responsibilities

Reasons why

Today we are surrounded by a whole new range of materials which have opened up exciting possibilities and introduced highly sophisticated techniques of production. The advent of plastics, in particular, has probably had a greater and a more immediate impact on our lives than can be claimed for any other material used by our parents. The expanding field of synthetic materials, together with new concepts of construction, have not only invigorated the thinking of designers, architects and artists, but have posed new questions and stimulated new attitudes and values. Yet, can any concern for these new horizons be seen in schools? Are we even awake to the new problems and possibilities? Is the traditional use of clay, wood and metal still of value to children whose future lies in the twenty-first century? Can the old values and techniques have any meaning in a world of 'Lego' and 'Airfix' kits, of 'Knock-down' and inflatable furniture?

If we are convinced of the need for children to experience and exploit contemporary 'materials', are we satisfied with the opportunity we give them? Are we even sure that the opportunity we do provide is a valid experience at all?

In order to establish a basis for 'craft' activities and the reason for including 'materials' within the school curriculum today in terms applicable to our particular position in our particular school, we need to remind ourselves of the role that these materials play in our society.

If we look at man's creative energy and industry, we must acknowledge his need and facility to build and construct, whether for utility or for his own fulfilment. But why? What is the driving force behind that energy, a force that consumes more time, resources, and material than any other human activity? Is the answer a simple, yet fundamental one – man's need to 'extend' his own capacity?

Since his first tentative efforts to control and alter his environment, man has looked for ways and means of improving or 'extending' his own performance. He cannot carry very much or very far, so he has developed the sledge, the cart, and the freight carrier. He cannot see too well, so he has invented the magnifying glass, the telescope and now radar. Even the computer can be seen as an 'extension' of man – this time of his capacity to calculate and analyze. The list is endless, yet the basic impulse seems constant. From his fountain pen to his tooth brush, from his motor bike to his television set, all are in some way and in some measure a result of man's continuing

The development of new technologies and the introduction of synthetic materials open up new possibilities and challenge our imagination.

Reproduced by courtesy of Brecht-Einzig Ltd.

Is the traditional concept of handicraft still pertinent to children whose future lies in the twenty-first century?

Products sold and photographed by Habitat, England.

Photograph by Barnaby's Picture Library.

Photograph by John Topham Ltd.

Since his first tentative efforts to control and alter his environment, man has looked for ways and means of 'extending' and improving his own performance.

Photograph by Derek Pratt.

By combining his inventiveness, his knowledge and his familiarity with materials, man continues to 'extend' his total understanding.

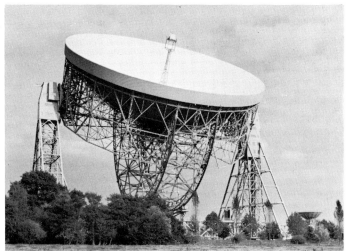

need to 'extend'. To be more efficient, to improve his own condition in relation to his environment, is as basic an impulse and as vital to his existence today as it ever was.

This need to 'extend' is not, however, the complete picture. There is another equally important aspect of the basic impulse of making – this time a more personal one. It is man's apparent need to 'extend' his own thoughts and ideas – to 'say something about himself'. The exquisite geometry of a Celtic brooch, the powerful carving of the Easter Islanders, the elegance of Georgian silver, the precision of a Brancusi sculpture, or even the individual way we dress, reveal something of our culture and of 'ourselves'. The totem pole, the icon and the monument have had a meaning for man beyond that of utility – they show something of his thoughts, his fears and his aspirations. The very fact that we feel something when we admire a Windsor chair, or marvel at a Michelangelo sculpture, reminds us that our senses respond to more than the utility of an object.

If the satisfaction of man's need to 'extend' in various ways is as vital to his existence as the balance of the air he breathes, then education is charged with an important responsibility. If this premise is accepted, there follow questions such as 'In what context should children meet materials?' 'How should the contemporary picture of advancing technology and synthetic materials be reflected in 'craft' activities?'

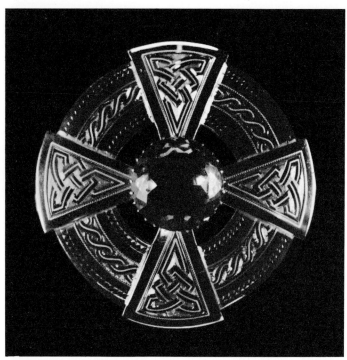

This exquisite geometry serves more than its function of a brooch.

Photographs by Scott Adie Ltd.

Man's command of materials goes beyond utility and reaches for something which expresses his own culture and personality.

Georgian coffee pot. Lord Bristol's collection.

Maiastra by Brancusi. Courtesy of the Tate Gallery, London.

As individuals with our own aspirations we continue to say just that!

Photograph by Spectrum Colour Library.

Photograph by Keystone Press Agency Ltd.

Through materials man has conveyed his fears, his aspirations: even his sense of drama.

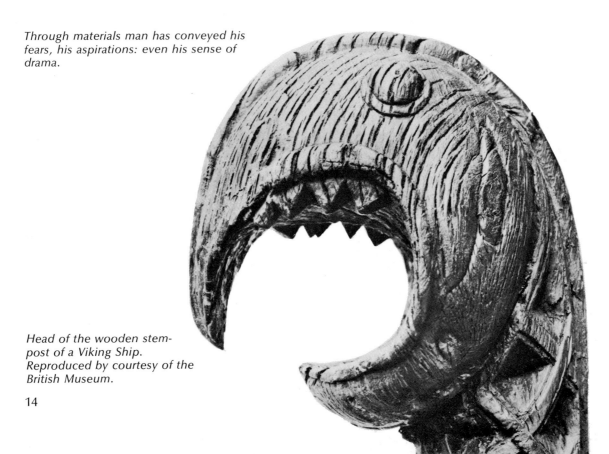

Head of the wooden stempost of a Viking Ship. Reproduced by courtesy of the British Museum.

Can we deny our feelings in how we use materials?

The Virgin and Child with the young St. John the Baptist by Michelangelo. Reproduced by courtesy of the Royal Academy.

Change and Alienation

'We live in a changing society' – how often have we heard this remark, sometimes to the point of exasperation and annoyance. Yet the basic truth is inescapable, the world cannot go back or even stand still – it must go on! Today, it is the very pace of that movement and change that complicates and sometimes contradicts our attitudes. Contemporary technology is advancing so fast that often a new material or a new machine, such as an aeroplane, becomes obsolete before it has had a chance to prove itself. The threat of technology 'taking over' is real enough. If, however, we are to master our discoveries and direct technology to serve us, rather than the reverse, *we must be aware of the consequences of our own actions.*

One real problem that is emerging as a result of the technological society is *alienation.* The growing separation between man and the materials and artifacts he uses, is damaging not only his judgement but weakening his very understanding of the world that surrounds him. How many of us realize the significance of a transistor, appreciate the potential of pre-stressed concrete, or know how our polythene washing-up bowl was produced? Although it may not be necessary to know how a clock works in order to tell the time, an awareness that polythene will melt if put on a hot stove might extend the life of our washing-up bowl!

When the materials used were fewer, and man worked materials by hand and simple tools, he grew to have an almost intuitive understanding of the nature and quality of those materials. He was in direct control. Both craftsmen and laymen had closer personal contact with the materials and the very processes which lay behind the things they used.

The story of the small boy who really thought that the shape of fish fingers indicated the true shape of fish, brings home to us *a responsibility that education must accept* – to familiarize children with the materials that constitute their environment today. This is, perhaps, a more urgent priority than ever before.

In what context, then, should children meet materials? If we accept the inclination of child and man alike to build 'extensions' to his own thoughts – then surely we are given a clue to our question. The introduction to the handling and using of materials should stem from the child's own interests and ideas. This does not evade adult responsibility or imply a free-for-all – far from it! To respect the child's own concern, to support and assist his endeavours, is no mean task.

In addition, the need to provide a 'working atmosphere'

Inspiration or folly – has man lost control of technology?

Photograph by British Aircraft Corporation.

in which the freedom to experiment is balanced by an awareness of a social responsibility, does not suggest a teacher who has opted out. But if we acknowledge the child's own imagination and inventiveness as the growth point, then the tragedy of one secondary school, situated among a complex of tall, centrally-heated flats, will be avoided. Here, in metalwork classes, the boys were making, not without some scepticism, a poker!

How should the contemporary picture of advancing technology and synthetic materials be related to 'craft' activities? This question has to be met, in the first instance, not so much by a blind acceptance of everything that is new, as by a considered reappraisal of traditional practice and values.

In past cultures, the varied systems of apprenticeship and studio 'schools' provided a notable education. Though these strict and conservative organizations were rather restrictive in character, the close association with the master, the daily absorption of material and process, produced not only work of unqualified craftsmanship but men of repute and quality. In our time the Bauhaus retained something of the Craft Guild's structure and philosophy. Walter Gropius, chief architect of the Bauhaus, was, however, able to inject into static craft traditions a momentum relevant to the twentieth century. The Bauhaus belief lay in rediscovering the very nature and potential of materials; of exploiting to the full, current technology and expertise; in relating their design to current problems. Gropius states, 'Our underlying principle lay in the belief that design is neither a material nor an intellectual affair, but simply the stuff of life.'

The challenge then for all craft teachers is to exploit the possibilities of a curriculum which acknowledges the place of 'materials', and to present those 'materials' in a way *relevant* and *meaningful* to the children of *today*.

Photograph by Camera Press Ltd.

Alienated by machine tool and automated process – how can we preserve a personal contact with materials?

In the Bauhaus the use of materials was tied to a contemporary understanding of society – its purpose and its potential.

Cesca chair designed by Marcel Breuer. Photograph by John Cook.

17

Chapter 2

Children, Materials and Tools

Richard is nine and built this 'house' in the freedom of his garden at home. At first sight, the 'house' appears haphazard and does not indicate a particular design or reveal a high standard of craftsmanship. Yet if we can put aside adult preoccupations for a moment and look at 'Richard's house' in more detail, certain features have a message for us:

(a) Richard did not preconceive the image or the plan of his house in a formal working drawing. The house grew by the coming together of material and ideas.

(b) His main concern has been bringing to life his personal idea rather than following any correct craft procedure.

(c) The division of the house into rooms, and the 'exact' nature of the household arrangements including a solid fuel oven that works, illustrate a 'particular' attitude. *Things had to be right*. Right, that is, in *his own terms*. For if we were to assess Richard's structure in terms of building conventions, we would have difficulty in finding anything right!

(d) Richard's use of advice, help and example were constantly related to his particular problem *at that time*. 'How can I fix this?' 'Do you think I should put the window here or over there?'

Supported by the tolerance of his parents, with ample space and a supply of 'found' material, Richard has carried out his ideas with confidence and conviction. Richard, however, is not unique in this obvious energy and persistence to construct and build.

In an Adventure Playground at Lewisham, boys of different ages have constructed their own tree houses, dens and palaces. These early structures by children are significant not for their craftsmanship or aesthetic quality, but because they serve a basic impulse – to give a *physical form to ideas*, ideas that are the reality in which children 'live'.

Many people would accept the constructions of Richard and the boys at Lewisham as a normal product of play and leave it at that. But can we leave it at this? Surely we should harness that obvious energy and conviction to the child's own educational benefit within the school framework.

Our attitude to play and its relation to learning is largely reflected in how we, as adults, use the word – 'Stop playing about' or 'go away and play'. Play is usually seen as a childish activity which somehow loses respectability as we

Richard's house. Its lesson for us lies beyond an adult concept of aesthetics or craftsmanship.

An association of ideas and materials that through experiment and thoughtful consideration, went beyond an intuitive response.

Things had to be right. This outside fire, which served an inside oven, was rebuilt many times until it worked.

get older. Dismissed as negative or at best therapeutic, play is rarely seen as an agent of learning beyond the lower reaches of the primary school. Yet the evidence of learning, of realizing new relationships, of understanding new possibilities, in Richard's constructions is clear. The house was modified not once, but many times; additions and

Part of an adventure playground at Lewisham where old timbers are rearranged to create a new environment.

As much by instinct as by design, children 'extend' their world by using the very materials that it offers.

20

Richard's cars show not only his inventiveness, but a keen sense of observation.

improvements were made; detail became more developed, exact and refined.

At another time, Richard designed and built these cars, and in his determination to make them work, he began to *explore* and *extend* simple mechanical and scientific concepts. Play is closely connected with all types of exploration and finding out. Even as adults when we meet a new situation, whether it be a new material, a new environment or even a new human relationship, we explore, examine and test it. It is through this process that we come to terms with the new material or the new social contact.

Many people who can see the value of Richard's house will, nevertheless, be sceptical about transferring this type of experience to the school. Still more, they will not know where to start and will have doubts about the degree of freedom that personal ideas should be allowed in the classroom and workshop.

With encouragement and support a child's natural ability to build can become a very positive agent in his total understanding.

Men, materials and tools – as basic an issue today as it has ever been.

This middle school in the Isle of Wight has a combined Art and Craft area for the use of the whole school. An interesting project, which is closely related to Richard's house, stems from the attempt of these children to construct a 'den'. These boys visited a local forestry plantation, and brought back to school a good supply of palings. They were determined to build a cabin, and were given a site and allowed a short time (normally a personal option) at the end of each day. Rather than dictate the shape of the cabin, the teacher allowed the boys to carry out their own ideas, even at times at the expense of failure. They tried out a number of structures and methods of building, learning from their mistakes and adding to their understanding of construction. Finally they arrived at the post and lintel principle in which they saw the solution to the problem. Their experience illustrates Pestalozzi's words, 'Man must not learn and then do, but learn from what he does.'

A workshop environment that is sympathetic to children's ideas. This is a first priority.

Waste materials are more than a visual stimulus, they provide a base from which ideas can form and grow. These pictures show a robot and a mechanical hand.

In this workshop in a comprehensive school in Gloucestershire, the teacher puts children's ideas at a premium and sees his basic role as providing a stimulating and responsive environment. He seeks 'to create an environment of enquiry, discovery and inventiveness where each child can bring his ideas, learning and questions and explore them through material in his own way, but supported with help.'

The opportunities provided by this specialist workshop have been enriched by a mass of found material, natural and man-made. This includes industrial waste, obsolete television sets, parts of engines and many other objects. These materials are more than a visual stimulus; they provide the basis for the children's ideas to form and grow. The vivid nature of their work supports the contention that children's imagination and inventiveness must not be overladen by adult concepts of skill and craftsmanship.

Tools, Skill and Craftsmanship

Many people are nervous at the thought of young children using tools. Concern for safety, a feeling of personal inadequacy, or the simple issue of economics are usually enough for many teachers, particularly in the primary sector, to regard the problem of children using tools as one they could well do without. Even from the age of five or six, however, children will respond to simple tools and display considerable facility and persistence with them. With guidance they are able to attain a sufficient measure of control, enough to encourage their ideas to mature and flourish. The determination of the child who grasps this new opportunity to express his ideas is inescapable.

It is interesting to note in the unashamed naïvety of children's early work, a lack of the adult craftsman's concern with precise and exact detail. Theirs is a real and precious concern to effect ideas and communicate feelings – *to say something* and extend their world.

Although the use of resistant materials in primary education is a feature in some schools today, it cannot be claimed that the use of these materials is widespread, or that their potential is fully realized. Not until the child reaches secondary school, and then normally only for boys, is real contact with resistant materials and tools made. Yet if man's instinct to use materials and develop skill in handling tools stems from an early age, why frustrate this development until the child is eleven? By waiting until then, do we not ignore a fertile basis for learning and deny children a means of expression and self realization?

The absurd distinction between girls' crafts and boys' crafts that still exists in many schools, particularly secondary schools, defies explanation! This outworn attitude seems more appropriate to the social confines of the Victorian drawing room than to the comparative liberation of the twentieth century. It is a strange paradox that although for many years we have held in esteem male cooks and fashion designers, only recently have women become serious contenders in the field of industrial design and architecture. The social expectations of girls and boys in respect to their contact with 'resistant materials' relates more closely to vocational than educational observation. Surely this absurd prejudice and discrimination must be laid to rest. Our responsibility should be to move ahead of social expectations, to point to new possibilities and potential and to offer the opportunity to use resistant materials to *all* children.

Even at six years old children can show an eager response to simple tools.

One of the factors that has circumscribed the attitude to children and their use of resistant materials stems from the traditional preoccupation with the 'crafts'. Since the inception of the crafts into the curriculum, the idea that the learning of a craft skill is a worthy objective has remained. This, together with an adult concept of craftsmanship, became the prime objective of work with children. The cherished saying 'If a thing is worth doing, it's worth doing

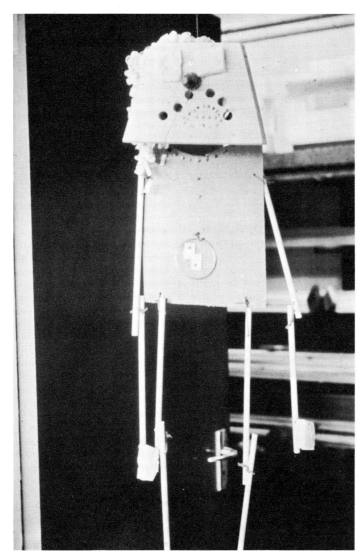

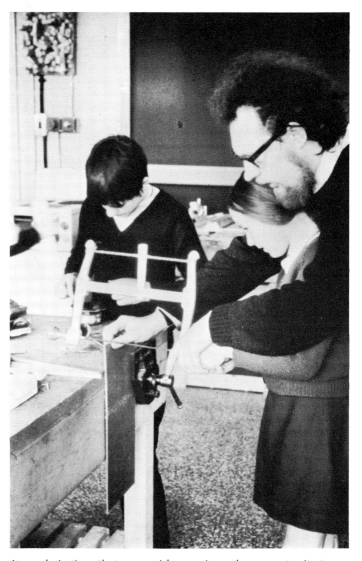

In the unashamed naivety of children's early constructional work, their imagery remains strong – how can we ensure that it is not lost?

It surely is time that more girls are given the opportunity to handle tools and materials.

well' reflects this thinking. Yet the saying can only have real meaning if we are sure that the 'thing' being done is 'worth doing'. Also, we need to allow ourselves more time to examine by whose criteria is 'well'.

Our concept of craftsmanship is more often than not adult-based and related to outmoded craft rituals. The artifacts we ask children to make often reflect adult interests or are simply a vehicle for a craft technique. Yet nearly all teachers, somewhere in their philosophy of education, would claim concern for the development of the individual child. A concern which is nevertheless often translated into getting children to accept our idea, our way, our standard. This is not to suggest that craft skills should be overlooked or considered irrelevant. Clearly they should not, for without the ability to direct the tool, the idea can never be resolved in the tangible form of

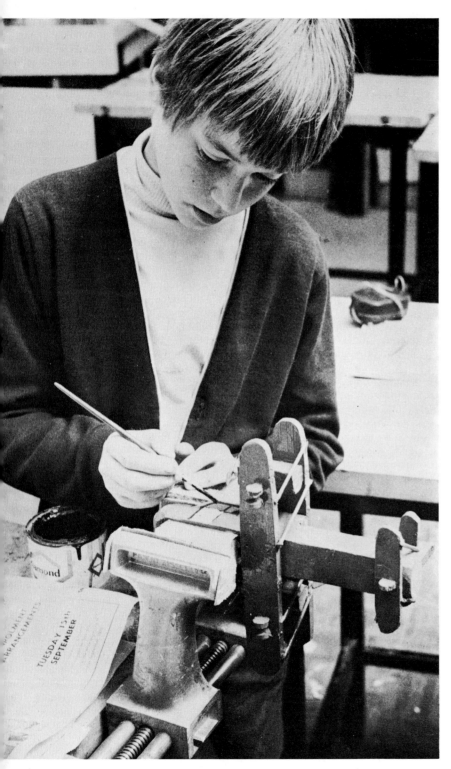

material. Certainly children's ideas can be frustrated as much by lack of tool skill and limited knowledge of processes, as they can by a situation in which craft skills are taught in preference to, and above, all else. What is needed is not an abject rejection of traditional craft skills, but rather respect for a new relationship, a relationship between the idea being pursued and the development of the skills necessary for its realization. The task is to seek a proper balance.

Summary

Many examples could be cited to illustrate the vitality of children's work with resistant materials. The evidence of children's enthusiasm to use tools, to build their idea in real terms, is clear enough.

Before we examine some of the practical issues involved, and the possible avenues of development, can we draw together the thesis so far put forward.

> That we should respect the native interest of most children, whether eight, eleven or thirteen years of age, whether boys or girls, to handle and utilize resistant materials.
> That recognition of this concern be directed towards the support of the child's own imagination and inventiveness.
> That the presentation of material should reflect the contemporary scene and allow for the breadth of children's curiosity.
> That the understanding and acquisition of manipulative skills be considered in conjunction with the pupils' ideas and consequent problems.

The task of the teacher must be to seek a proper balance between children's ideas and the development of the skills necessary for the realization of these ideas.

Chapter 3

Problems and Possibilities

A Choice of Materials

'Miss, this metal is too thick, it won't cut!'

'Sir . . . Is this really wood, sir?'

The problems of these two children reveal not only the frustration that can arise from trying to work with an inappropriate material, but also something of the confusion that results from the contemporary explosion of synthetic and man-made materials. The range of materials available today is immense and presents us with an immediate challenge – which shall we use? For clearly we have neither the time, money nor space to do justice to all.

On what basis can this choice be made? While economy and lack of space remain strong and insistent pressures, they should surely not dictate and define our selection. From our discussion so far, however, three considerations emerge which could well influence our decision:

(a)   That the materials chosen should be *convenient* and suitable for children to express and realize their own ideas.

(b)   That the range of material presented should promote a growing understanding of the *differences* between materials in terms of character and constructional potential.

(c)   That the choice of materials should include those with contemporary relevance and meaning.

Applying this criterion, it becomes more than obvious that while oak, cast iron, nylon and granite might demonstrate some of the differences between materials, it is doubtful if children, even at thirteen, would find them particularly sympathetic or see an immediate relevance to their ideas.

At eight or nine many children become frustrated if 'too much has to be done to the material' before they can get to their idea. They need materials which are quick to respond to their energy and enterprise; materials that will feed the imagination and build confidence. *Materials that are thin in section, are relatively easy to cut, are pliable or can be shaped or bent without too much trouble.*

We must acknowledge also the level of the child's own physique, control and co-ordination, by providing materials that extend and demand new skill, yet remain within his or her reach. The frustration caused by trying to saw heavy section timber or drive a nail through hardwood, does little beyond cause a loss of interest and a disintegration of ideas.

27

A six year-old at work on expanded Polystyrene with a hot wire cutter. Photograph by John Hunnex.

Working with soft iron. This is easily cut even by young children and can be shaped with the fingers. Photograph by John Hunnex.

28

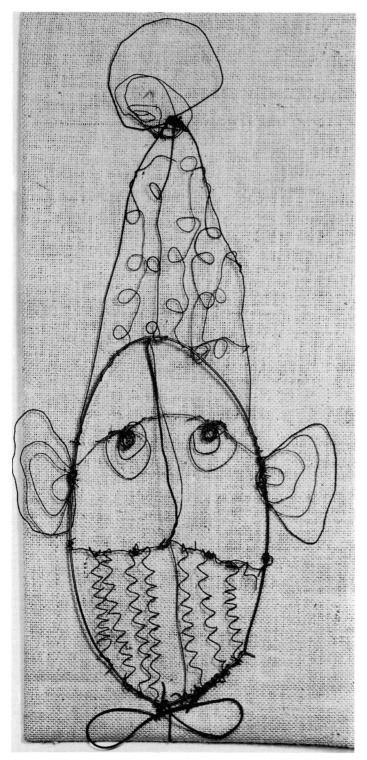

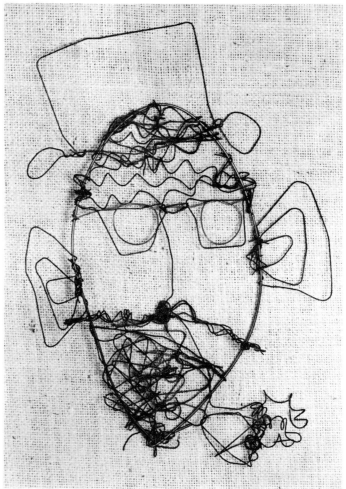

Two faces made from soft iron wire by a child aged eleven. Photograph by John Hunnex.

As we have already observed, children of this age are not particularly concerned with an adult concept of 'permanence' or making something 'of lasting value'. Their concerns and values are immediate, and their preoccupation changes with every new event and opportunity. While there is no *constant* image or standard to which they work, they do have standards, standards which are peculiar and valid for their idea at that particular time. Standards that grow as much by observation and personal experience as by dictate or subjection to a 'set of rules'.

29

The eight year-old has little or no special regard for 'new' materials. He will work as happily, and often with more imagination, with 'found' or 'scrap' material as with new, prepared material from an accepted stockist or county supplier. Offcuts from local firms and businesses such as shop fitters, builders, sign makers, sheet metalworkers, light engineering, toy manufacturers and packaging firms are invaluable. A visit to a radio and television repair shop, a cycle shop, even a chat to a shoemaker, electrician or plumber can provide not only a range of materials but an assortment of interesting shapes, forms and textures. Materials which by their very interest can stimulate and promote ideas.

Another source of material beyond the traditional stockist or the 'yellow pages', is provided, of course, by nature, in the wood, on the common, on the seashore and lakeside, the quarry, rockface and cliff. The rich harvest that children can collect from a walk on the beach illustrates the immediate association that they make with material through shape, texture and colour. Ideas for development spring from 'seeing an idea' in a found form, and if the original stone, branch or piece of driftwood was found by the child, then his idea will be more meaningful as a result.

An interesting bracelet made by bending soft wire.

A robot which has been made entirely from miscellaneous scrap.

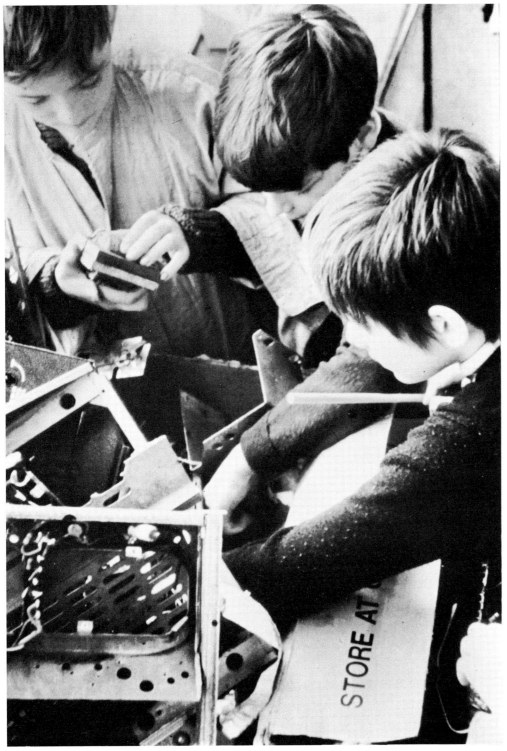

Children searching through a box full of scrap.

Finding a new relationship and a new context.

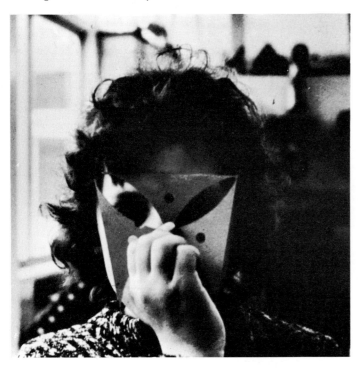

32

Apart from sources of found material, whether from factory, scrapyard or from nature herself, we should not overlook or undervalue those materials that stem from the child's own immediate world of play. A classroom or workshop that ignores the potential of 'Lego' and 'Meccano', for instance, denies its pupils many opportunities to build and construct – to discover mechanical and structural elements. The use of commercially available construction kits will be dealt with more fully later on, but it is sufficient here to say that if the development of children's imagination and inventiveness is a prime objective, then these 'materials' are invaluable if not essential.

The full benefit of using commercially available construction kits has yet to be realized in the classroom and workshop. Photograph by John Hunnex.

Using these 'materials' images and constructional concepts are conceived together. Photograph by John Hunnex.

A working model which includes its own friction drive power system.

The use of Meccano offers many constructional and mechanical opportunities.

Later on, towards thirteen, with increased age and maturity, a greater ability and understanding of materials is possible. Different values and expectations emerge. There is a greater degree of tool control, and new skills can be attempted. A regard for new standards begins, and a new understanding and awareness of quality develops, alongside the pupil's own growing values and attitudes.

Our choice of materials for the older age group needs to reflect their interest in scale, in precision and in attention to detail. The first teenage responses to fashion and to consumer spending will also necessitate an approach and provision of materials sympathetic to the current 'scene'. At twelve or thirteen the child's curiosity is no less in evidence than in the earlier years. It will, however, now be more 'specific' and particular. Interest in 'how things work' or 'how things come about' goes beyond a cursory examination. Parts of machines – an engine or watch – will serve to arouse and maintain this new interest in man's ingenuity and inventiveness with materials; they will awake a new understanding and deepen a new awareness of the potential of material.

As with mechanical forms, so with electrical components and circuitry. Electricity, while not strictly a material itself, cannot be harnessed to much effect without materials, and in our society today an appreciation of the influence and significance of electricity and electronics must be valid.

As the child approaches adolescence, so his attitude to adult behaviour and concepts changes. The use of machine tools becomes more than a novelty – it stands as a symbol of a change in status and adult acceptance. With suitable materials, machining in simple terms is quite within the capacity of the older pupil, as is also controlled casting of metals and the use of resins and glassfibre.

Concrete and the associated materials of sand and cement, brick and insulation block, provide another ideal range of materials for the upper age group. As yet, the creative possibilities of these materials of the builder and civil engineer have only been touched on in schools, yet their future use must be assured. Relatively cheap and easy to use, they reflect not only an adult world but, in terms of texture, scale and constructional potential, a new range of possibilities to be explored.

Girls, and indeed boys as well, often develop a keen interest in jewellery at this age which, if associated with an introduction to non-ferrous metals, might well encompass enamels and simple stone-setting.

With increased age come greater control and more specific demands.

Sources of materials will always present problems, not least in terms of capital and storage space (which we shall discuss later). Yet with determination and a little imagination most of these problems can be, if not overcome, certainly minimized. By taking advantage of the materials within the local environment, and those provided by business and industry, much can be obtained at a relatively low cost. The only firm criteria for the choice of material must derive from recognizing and responding to the combination of the child's native ability and skill and his or her developing interests. Above all the range of materials selected should arouse interest and suggest imaginative and inventive ideas.

The contemporary world of technology is rich in materials ready to stimulate and feed ideas.

Richard, aged nine, adding an electric circuit to one of his cars.

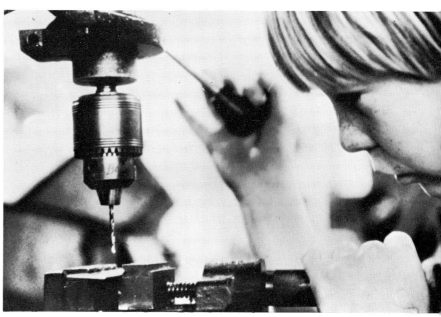

The use of machine tools can add a new dimension to working with constructional materials.

Carvings made from old kiln bricks.   *A head carved from a single brick.*

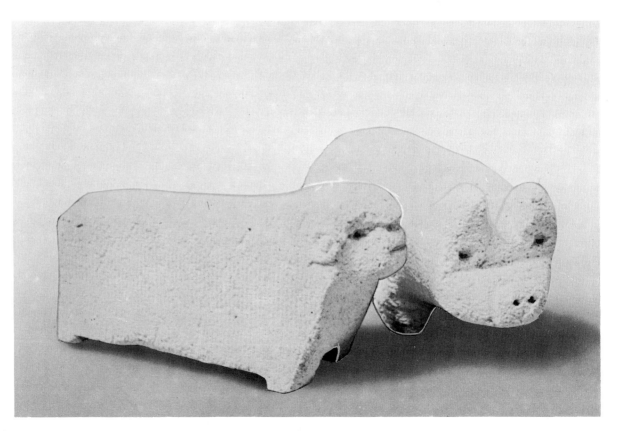

Concrete, a material that has yet to be fully appreciated for its creative potential.

MATERIALS	DESCRIPTION	SOURCE
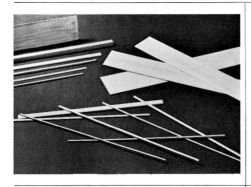	**Balsa Wood.** All sections and some block. Suitable for carving and construction for younger children. Model-making for the older group.	Materials stockists. Also some packaging from Asia and S. America is made from balsa wood.
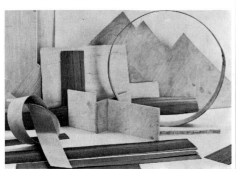	**Ply** 0.5 to 5.0 m. birchfaced. Thinner sections are very flexible and can be made into 3-dimensional forms. Thicker sheets have all-round usefulness and are easier to nail than hardboard. **Veneer.** Small collection for decorative work.	Materials stockists and packaging firms generally, ie. tea cases. Materials stockists and possible offcuts from cabinet makers.
	**Softwood.** Prepared and rough sawn sections. Prepared thinner sections more suitable for younger age group.	Timber stockists plus offcuts from builders, joiners, demolition firms, storage and packaging firms.
	**Hardwood.** Generally for older age group only. **Mild** hardwood such as Obeche, Mahogany, Meranti. Prepared sections will avoid waste and frustration. **Other Wood.** Driftwood, twigs and small branches. Orchard thinnings, etc. Fencing staves.	Hardwood merchants plus offcuts from joiners and shop fitters, cabinet makers and furniture firms. Seashore and river creek, countryside, wood and copse, orchards and forestry sites.

	**Metal** – Wire and foil. Range of soft iron and galvanized wire. Brass and gilding metal wire for older group doing jewellery. Welding rods $\frac{1}{16}''-\frac{1}{8}''$ dia. also very useful. Small amount of foil, steel, brass and aluminium. Easily cut with scissors. Useful for all ages.	Materials stockists and makers of lampshades and novelties.
	**Metal.** Sheet and strip and tube. Tin plate up to 2–4 gauge easily cut with shears and joined by pop-riveting or soldering (for older group). Steel sheet – mild steel up to $\frac{1}{16}''$ small amount only. Small stock of brass and gilding metal to 20 gauge. Bright mild steel strip small sections that can be drilled and riveted. Steel tube. Round and squared pieces for older pupils.	Material stockists plus scrap merchants. Useless offcuts from engineering and light metal fabricators. Pressings very useful. Bicycle and pram manufacturers.
	**Other Metal materials** – linkages and mechanisms, engine parts. Aluminium alloy 'Kayem' for casting. Zinc alloy for casting (the use of 'Petrobond' casting sand is recommended).	'Meccano'. Scrap merchants, garages and general purpose workshops. Watch and clock makers. Old typewriters and sewing machines.

MATERIALS	DESCRIPTION	SOURCE
	**Plastic** – Thermoplastic (i.e. heat softening). Expanded Polystyrene tiles and block up to 6" thick. Easily cut and shaped.	Stockists plus scrap. Packaging firms, interior decorators, insulation firms.
	Rigid PVC and Polythene sheet and Acylic for cutting and heat forming. Older pupils in particular.	Vacuum forming firms, plastic fabricators and stockists.
	PVC tube. (Drainpipes.)	Builders merchants and ventilation contractors.
	Other Plastics – Resins – Polyester casting and laminating using simple 'Vinamold' Wax and TIN plate moulds.	Stockists. Also glassfibre firms, ie. boatbuilders.
	Granules – Polythene and Polystyrene for tile making.	Stockists. Scrap material can also be used.
	**Stone** and other composite material. Soft Sandstone – chalk. Small stones and soft rock. Handmade soft bricks. Insulation block, 'Durox', 'Siporex'. Ballast. Sand, cement aggregates and various stone.	Quarries and rockface, seashore and hillside. Demolition firms. Old derelict houses. Builders merchants and building sites. Quarries and monumental masons.
	Other useful material – Electrical components.	Television and radio dealers. Government surplus.
	Construction kits. Bilofix, Lego, Meccano. Small electric motor.	Stockists.

Chapter 4

Construction and Processes of Fabrication

Traditionally, when children were introduced to wood and metal (usually isolated from one another!), they were given a diet of prescriptive exercises. The reason for this generally offered by teachers contained the belief 'that until the skills and processes are mastered, nothing worthwhile can be produced'. This view, held until recently by the majority of specialist handicraft teachers, stems logically from their own training and background. But it is a view that is largely conditioned by thinking of craft education as a form of vocational training. This was reflected in much of the work in many schools, which really was little more than a watered down apprenticeship course. In these prescriptive courses children's ideas had little place – the acquisition of tools, skills and the knowledge of working processes being all-important.

Recently, the value of children designing and developing their own ideas has been more fully appreciated, yet often the traditional rigid attitude to skills and processes remains. If children are to design and develop their own ideas, it must be appreciated that to insist on a measure of skill and ability to perform certain processes as a prerequisite to designing, is to misunderstand the nature of children's ideas and how they can be encouraged.

Children's ideas and designs invariably go beyond their own knowledge and capacity to handle materials. This in itself provides the teacher with the opportunity to bring the child to new skills and understanding in a way that springs from the child's ideas, rather than from a prenotion of the teacher. Clearly there will be times when, in order to move children on to other forms and ideas, it is necessary to present new ways of handling materials, new possibilities, and even new materials. But this must be to stimulate and provide potential for new ideas, not simply to instil new knowledge and develop new skill.

An early concept which it is important for children to grasp, is the realization that there are only three basic ways by which 'form' can be produced.

By wastage – change coming about through the removal of material from the initial form, as in carving, rasping, machining etc.

By addition – forms arising from the joining together of separate pieces of material.

By redistribution – change coming about by the material being redeployed over a new area – as in casting, raising, or in the simple development of sheet material. Material is neither removed from nor added to the original form.

Clearly these three ways of creating form are often combined with one another in a final idea – yet the concept of these three possibilities is a simple one for children to understand and apply to the problem of 'how they might do something'. Likewise, the concept could well be used by the teacher as a platform from which materials could be examined.

Is the teaching of tool skills the first priority?

Here the teacher is demonstrating new skills as they become necessary to the development of children's own ideas.

A second concept which deserves consideration concerns *construction*. Traditionally, construction has been married to techniques, to established methods of jointing and fabrication. Unfortunately the preoccupation with 'correct procedure and method' often means that the fundamental purpose of construction is missed.

For construction is about controlling movement. If we look at almost any product made from resistant materials, we will see at varying levels a regard for preventing, limiting or permitting movement. A deck chair, a guitar, a bicycle, in fact almost all man's artifacts, represent structures that are rigid at certain moments, but also need to be flexible or have movement as a deliberate requirement of their construction, as in a pair of scissors. Though this may seem an obvious point, it can help to direct attention back to the purpose of construction – a point from which teachers and children can discuss and plan appropriate constructions for their ideas. Left to themselves, young children will devise construction by trial and error, and as their demands are usually short term, they are pleased enough if the structure holds together – and nails are banged in until it does!

The fundamental issue – the need to facilitate, limit or prevent movement.

Photograph by Keystone Press Agency Ltd.

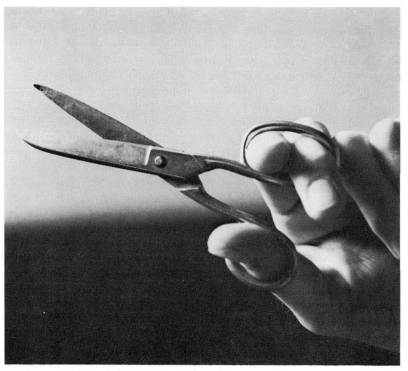

Photograph by Barnaby's Picture Library.

Photograph by Barnaby's Picture Library.

Photograph by Camera Press Ltd.

Photograph by Spectrum Colour Library.

47

There is little immediate understanding or anticipation by children of the various pressures, strain, weight or forces that their structure will have to face. The teacher must aim to arouse this awareness by demonstration, discussion and example. In this way the child can come to understand something of the problems of construction, and through this begin to apply himself to it, instead of using haphazard experiment and random trial and error.

The task of the teacher should be to present the *purpose and problem* of construction in association with possible solutions. He should see the possibilities for constructional experience in the children's problems and ideas, *rather than* prearrange construction exercises by choosing the problem and dictating the solution.

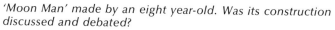

'Moon Man' made by an eight year-old. Was its construction discussed and debated?

Exploratory constructions using card.

48

How can I stop it falling down?

49

Purpose and problem – this is the real context of construction.

Hammer and nails – the final answer!

50

One of the continual problems of using resistant materials is the length of time necessary to bring an idea into tangible reality. As ideas are precious and need to be encouraged, anything that can be done to lessen the time spent in translating the idea without invalidating the craft opportunity must be considered. The use of modern synthetic adhesives can not only speed up glueing operations, but through their increased bonding strength can remove the necessity for some traditional jointing procedure.

The use of a 'pop riveter' and later on a spot welder can accelerate metal fabrication. The combination of a pillar drill and a dowelling jig can speed construction in any workshop. Later on, the use of commercially available 'Knock-down' fittings is an ideal solution to many construction problems and at the same time has an immediate relevance to contemporary production techniques.

A pop riveter – a useful addition to any workshop. Photograph by John Hunnex.

A pillar drill and dowelling jig in use. Photograph by John Hunnex.

Simple jigs can add new possibilities and speed production.

I have already mentioned the use of Meccano and similar construction kits. Their application in the workshop for the eight to thirteen age group is still gravely undervalued – not least in their capacity to awaken and alert interest in mechanisms. They are useful in the construction of ideas that have moving parts, that in some way operate and perform deliberate actions or movement – as in a crane, a model of a lifting bridge, or a go-kart. Because the child is not involved in the traditional craft sense – beyond the use of screwdriver and spanner – this does not invalidate the use of construction kits. The understanding and appreciation that children can absorb from handling and building with these materials is considerable – not least in the preliminary working out of initial ideas. They also have the advantage that they are not 'consumable' in the normal sense of craft materials!

Meccano is ideal for constructions that require moving parts.

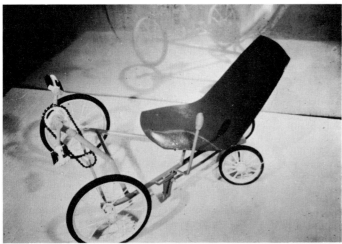

Designing and Developing Ideas

The illustrations we have already looked at show that children do have ideas and can design. Given encouragement and opportunity, this ability can not only blossom, but give a new impetus to their whole education. Although some of the benefits of children developing their own ideas and designing their own work are gradually being accepted and respected, the means of giving support, guidance and direction to children during the formation of their ideas and designs is still being argued. One important concept that is, however, fundamental to the design and development of ideas concerns the dependent relationship that exists between the desired *form*, the appropriate *material*, and the available *means* of production.

The very essence of using resistant materials relies on this obvious yet elusive relationship. Many students will have ideas and produce designs which are either impossible to make at all, or if they are, would be prohibitive in cost. The compromise that has to be made between what is desirable and what is possible is not a restriction on ideas, it is simply part of the process of resolving them. Just as some ideas will suggest the use of a specific material, so in turn the disciplines of the chosen material may suggest form and demand particular means of production. The available material and facilities may, in turn, suggest new ideas and new forms; they are essentially interwoven and reliant upon one another. An early realization of this relationship by children will defeat later frustration as a result of unworkable ideas, promote an acceptance of the need to anticipate and plan, and develop an awareness of the consequence of action, cause and effect. It must, therefore, be an early and persistent priority of any teacher whose concern is with developing children's ideas through the use of resistant materials.

Pedal toys made by students. How much did their early education help them?

A child's use of appropriate techniques and materials to achieve form.

Considering and Organizing Ideas

The starting point for ideas lies in a complex association of stimuli, experience and a facility to see new relationships. We can do much to help this by providing an environment that is vital, alive, invigorating, and full of visual and tactile reference, a changing museum of natural and man-made objects – from a crab shell to a carburettor. But once the germ of an idea settles in the child's mind, what can we do to aid its growth to the later stage when the design is ready for translation into its final material form? It is this *formative* stage that is probably the most critical in the development and realization of ideas. It is a time when ideas have to be 'turned over', 'worked out', 'discussed' both *within the individual* and through communication *with others*. To this end man has always used his graphic ability to good effect. Ideas have to be 'seen', to be 'put down', in order that they can be explored and examined. The role that sketching and drawing can play is unique and deserves the fullest attention.

From an early age children love to draw; drawing provides an extension to their own fantasies, a meeting ground between fantasy and reality, and a means of communicating feeling and understanding. In school this natural ability is all too often separated from 'making', and in the secondary school the isolation is often complete, with separate rooms and teachers for art, technical drawing and handicraft! If we are serious in our determination to employ resistant materials as part of children's creative education, this absurd *laissez-faire* attitude must be resolved. At present, the drawing in the art room is rarely connected with the development of 3-dimensional ideas. The drawing in the technical room is all too frequently constrained by compass, ruler and 2H pencil, and pays little attention to the development of ideas. The drawing in the workshop is usually trite, if it exists at all! Is it any wonder that children's imaginations suffer and that teachers find ideas hard to come by? Yet the opportunity

A changing museum. Its purpose is to pose questions and to stimulate ideas. Photograph by John Hunnex.

Children's drawings. Do we realize their potential?

remains; we have only to see its significance. We must respect children's drawings, encourage and lead them to the stage where their drawing can be a real medium of communication. Help must be given and opportunities provided. Drawing must be seen as an important element in the resolution of ideas and designs. It must not, however, be thought of as a 'separate stage', as something you do before 'making' and once done, that's it! Drawing must be seen as an integral part of the whole process of developing ideas, as something which can constantly be referred to, a link between thoughts, experiments and 'making'. It is not a separate study or activity. Children should *use* drawing, should be able to apply a mode of drawing to a particular idea; sometimes freehand, sometimes measured. Encouraged to see drawing as an element of planning and organizing their own thoughts, children's ideas will have a chance.

Drawing is not, of course, the only process through which ideas can be seen and resolved. There are many occasions when it is essential to handle the actual materials, other times when a model or mock-up is necessary. 'Seeing' an idea in three dimensions is a complex and difficult business, and anything that can prompt and help to bring the idea into sharper focus is valid. Experiments, tests and trials should be encouraged, the use of paper, card, balsa wood, clay, anything that is quick, flexible and relatively cheap should be used to mock up ideas, examine proportions and explore constructional problems.

In all this, whether drawing, making a model, searching for information, or discussing thoughts, the child is formulating and building up his design. Many teachers, though realizing the value of the preliminary work, do not allow enough time for it – feeling that the child must get on and make something! But if we are searching for a genuine creative education, time for thought and the consideration of ideas is essential.

Children's ideas in graphic form. Are we doing enough to help children realize their ideas?

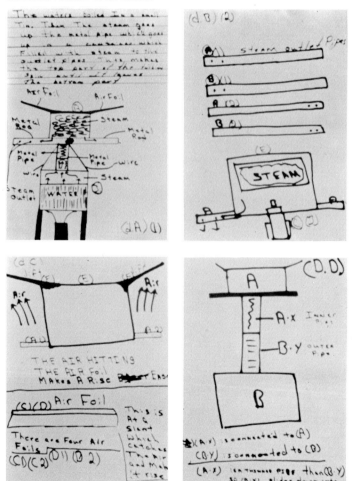

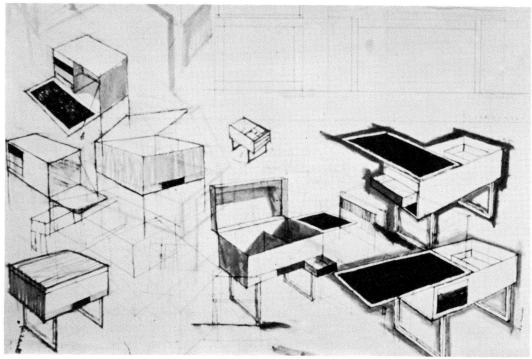

This student's design sheet presents a graphic discussion of ideas.

Model making helps to see an idea in three dimensions.

Chapter 5

Starting Points

'Where do I begin?' 'How can I get them going?' How often have we all asked these questions, if not of each other, then certainly of ourselves. There is probably no teacher, whatever his or her age, skill or experience, who has not asked at some time, 'How do I start?'

These questions are natural enough and indeed necessary to the continued growth of creative education, for if we knew all the answers, there would be no scope for new ideas. Moreover, as society changes, so do its children's values; their interests and response to stimulus alters and what worked with one class last year will not automatically succeed this year. Therefore a continual reappraisal and consideration of different starting points are needed and often essential to a teacher's growing awareness and understanding of the relationship he can forge between his pupils and the materials around them.

Although being dictated to can be very stultifying, working things out all by oneself is often no better. What we all need are initial thoughts and initial direction along a path we can recognize and handle. Here are some ideas that may provide possibilities for a beginning. They are not the complete journey, a course or a syllabus. They are deliberately not detailed, except in example. They are intended to bring into focus something of the landscape, not to draw a map – the journey is yours.

The Material

Perhaps the most obvious, yet often the most under-used starting point is the material itself. For the convenience of this discussion, we have divided the possibilities into two main areas:
(a) search, find and develop, (b) observation, examination and exploration.

Both 'ways in' stem from and reflect an appreciation of the innate human tendency to be curious and, at the same time, ask for an understanding by the teacher of the educational value that stems from *discovery* and *exploration* by their pupils.

Search, Find and Develop

The local environment of most schools, whether it is rural, on the coast or in an industrial complex, can often be a treasure chest of materials, both natural and man-made, *provided* we search for it. To begin with at least, you will probably need to initiate the search by:

A walk – to local woods, copse or common, along the shoreline, river or canal.

A visit – to local business and industry, ie. manufacturers, wood-yards, packaging firms, development schemes, building and demolition sites, government and public service maintenance depots, forestry plantations, mines, quarries, transport and marshalling yards, farms.

A collection – from home and workshop (parents, relations and community), rubbish tip and wasteland.

Whatever the range of material or objects (whether collected by an individual child, the teacher or by a whole class), one clear observation can usually be made – children tend to 'attach' themselves to a particular material or a specific object, often just a shape. This relationship is the vital clue, for the association means that a feeling has begun, a possibility, a meaning or an application has been seen. *The found materials are in themselves agents that stir the imagination.* If the teachers asks 'What is this?', 'Where has this come from?', 'What else could it do?', the children's own comments will follow – 'it looks like an angry dragon', 'a robot's head', 'a fire engine', 'headphones'. Such a discussion is often enough to start work – to develop and extend the 'seen' image or its use.

The blasé attitude of some children to familiar objects can usually be broken through by re-directing their observation through another means or dimension. The use of a magnifying glass; a strong light to project shadow and silhouette; observation through a camera lens (page 62); a careful drawing; even just taking things apart! All these will help to loosen the imagination and kindle ideas.

The defined form and the variety of shapes that found materials have, whether natural or man-made, is a beginning, a starting point. 'Found' material is cheap and full of unexpected possibilities, and it can lead a child to a new understanding of shape and form, to a new awareness of the potential of the material to make new images and serve other functions.

What else could these materials become? What ideas do they promote? Photographs by John Hunnex.

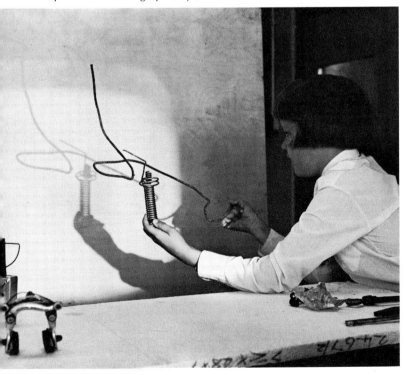

Search and find.

Scrap into ideas – humorous and dramatic. Photographs by John Hunnex.

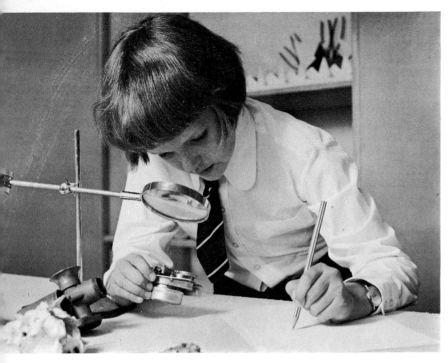

Having a closer look. Photograph by John Hunnex.

Observation, Examination and Exploration

An awareness of the physical potential of materials is vital to a child's deepening understanding of them. The physical nature of materials is, of course, unconsciously and intuitively observed during any normal process of making, shaping and assembling. However, by coupling this intuitive observation with empirical and rational experiment, it is possible to heighten a child's understanding of a material and bring him to a new level of awareness about its potential for him.

An appreciation of the relative strength of materials, their rigidity, their elasticity, their reaction to heat and water, their response to similar tools and adhesives, are but some of the specific qualities which ultimately all of us, whether children or adults, need to understand if a continuing appreciation of materials is to be maintained.

By appealing to the child's curiosity, by proposing a series of experiments, by simple yet leading questions such as 'How "tight" a bend can you make?', 'Can you scratch it with your fingernail?', 'What happens when you heat it?', 'Will it burn?' you can arouse curiosity and impress the imagination. The children's own questions will follow.

While much can be gained from examining a specific material on its own, be it card, plywood, tin plate or PVC, the benefits of understanding the relative values of materials is essential. For, from that understanding, discrimination can grow and a feeling of appropriateness mature. Opportunities to make comparisons *between* a range of different materials open up an awareness of the *particular* merits, the advantages and disadvantages of *specific* materials. Simple tests reveal the strongest, the most flexible, the softest, the most inflammable, and children being children, they will discover much more!

The example test card/record sheet on page 63 illustrates this simple yet direct starting point. When planning such a 'handout', room should be made for individual observations to come to the surface and subjective comment – 'Is it nice to handle?', 'What would *you* like to make with it?', 'Which is the best material?' – should be asked for.

Photograph by John Hunnex.

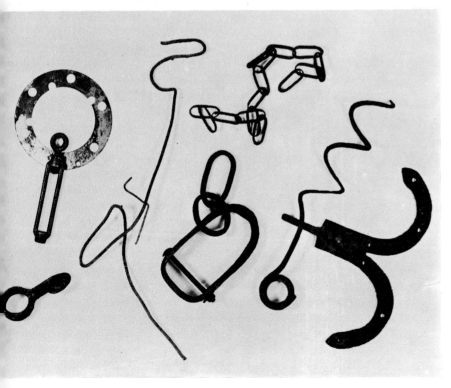

PLASTICS TEST CARD No.5

You have been given pieces of 3 different plastic materials
A) Acrylic   B) Polythene   C) P.V.C. - carry out the tests and
write in what you find out.

Which sample feels the coldest	Acrylic
Will any of the samples float	Polythene
Which sample will scratch the easiest	Polythene
Which sample is the least flexible (no heat to be used)	Acrylic
When you heat the samples over the strip heater which one was the best for bending into an L	P.V.C.
Which sample has a nasty (acrid) smell when it is burnt (one corner only)	P.V.C.
Which plastic would you use to make a wall bracket holder for a toothbrush	Acrylic or P.V.C.

An early structure showing a first appreciation of triangulation.

From these initial experiments and examination, a further realization can be made. Through a suitable challenge we can bring the child/pupil to a point where he begins to exploit the physical and constructional potential of the material.

'How high can you build a tower using just one sheet of paper?'
'How many bricks can you support 1½ in. above the ground, using 24 matchsticks?'

Questions such as these challenge the child's imagination and arouse his inventiveness. Apart from seeing and handling material within a specific context, he is also introduced, albeit in a limited sense, to construction; to the simple mathematics of structures and the economical use of material.

A balsa wood bridge showing the exploitation of a successive series of triangles.

63

Children need the chance to *exploit* their growing awareness of materials, and without this opportunity, the use of materials in schools will never realize its true educational potential. The 'test card' may be a start, but it is not enough; it must be followed up by opportunity.

Opportunities to exploit the context of materials need careful planning and sensitive presentation. While some children will respond to a direct challenge, others will not, and other 'starting points' may be more successful. The 'way in' to a child's appreciation of materials is often difficult to find, yet in reality seldom needs to be elaborate.

A thirteen year-old puts plywood to work as a seat.

Exploring the possibility of plywood.

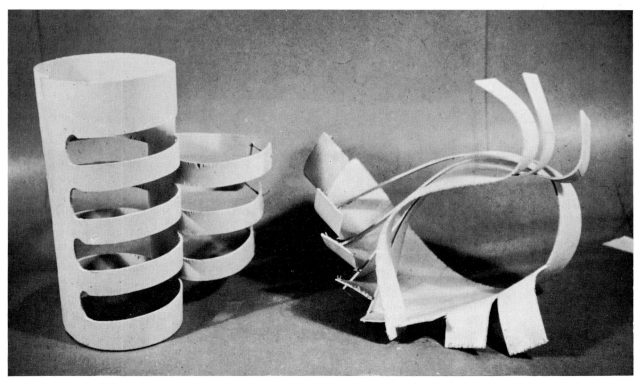

64

Three twelve year-old boys exploit their understanding of plywood.

65

Image and Idea

The opposite of working towards an idea from a specific material is a 'way of working' which *starts with an idea or image* and then progresses towards the appropriate material. This time, the materials are the agency through which ideas are achieved, rather than being the stimulus for the idea. It is a way of working which may be more suitable for some children than others, but is of benefit to everyone at some time.

Again, for convenience, we might see this 'starting point' as having two main areas of growth:

(a) the area of potential and possibility (something that *might* exist or happen)
(b) the area of reality and probability (something that is *likely* to exist or happen).

Both these starting points lean heavily on children's imagination, on their capacity to inspire fantasy, even on their ability to dream. Both areas demand of the teacher, tolerance and sensitivity. Respect for the fantastic and the unlikely, must parallel that for the reasonable and the useful.

A giant's piece of cheese.

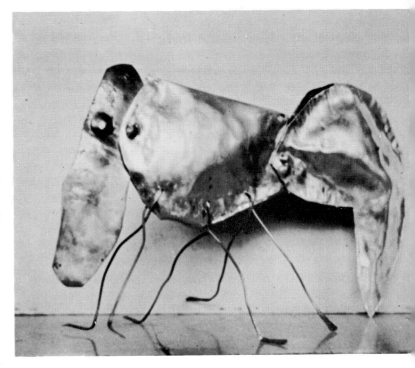

An insect made by an eleven year-old and a vulture made by an older student.

Potential and Possibility

The naïve world of 'make believe' and fantasy is often considered to be the child's prerogative. As we grow up, society impresses on us adult and rational responses as being the correct basis for belief and behaviour. Yet in all our dreams, whatever our age, the wonder of possibility and vividness of fantasy remain.

Alongside a recognition of the world of make believe we need an awareness, as teachers, of the central importance of *feeling* to the growth of a child's personal image or idea – be it a giant, a rocket or a castle in the sky. Ideas and personal images are precious, and stem as much from emotional responses as from intellectual rationalization.

The stimulus of a story, be it of strange people, unknown lands or events is often enough to 'start' the younger child. It is enough to allow the child to 'see' an image and to attach himself to it, be it a castle, a robot or a dog-exercising machine!

The older pupil will still respond to a flight of fantasy, but may well need reassurance from a group discussion to clarify his own ideas. Science fiction and the world of tomorrow are sure bets, while the opportunity to return to earlier forms of childhood fantasy is often also taken up.

It is interesting to note the 'greenhouse' construction of two fifteen year-old girls – is theirs a more advanced fantasy or a facile reality?

An interesting point about children's fantasy is often their disregard for scale. While specific details have 'to be right', the younger child doesn't seem concerned whether the scale of relative components of the idea are compatible. Is this further proof of the child's ability to hold the real and the imaginary in balance, and to alternate between either extreme as the idea permits? This facility of children to move at will from a state of fantasy to one of 'real' concern is perplexing to the teacher, who often sees the real and the imagined as separate thoughts. We have to recognize that if we intervene too heavily on the side of reality, we could dissolve the child's imagination – which clearly needs a continuing contact with fantasy.

The greenhouse!

If we remind ourselves of Richard's house we can see clearly his concern with real materials and specific detail, yet in fact his house is a product of his fantasy and it is through his imagination that it lives.

Wasn't this also the case of the pupil who built this 'Garden for a mouse' from metal. The inner involvement of the child could so easily have been broken by adult comments about proportion, or the fact that the mouse could escape, etc. More important than adult reality is the vivid nature of this child's work and his ability to see unfamiliar relationships – a basis of imagination.

Children's drawings often display ideas that can be taken up and explored further in resistant materials, for in their sketches, children gain an awareness of their own ideas and are able to discuss thoughts about them, both within themselves and with the teacher. From this they gain confidence, so that their drawings are not so much 'working drawings' as starting points from which they can move. For some, their drawings are indeed working plans – an implicit part in *their process* of transforming an idea into a tangible construction.

In the imagination everything has new potential, even mice!

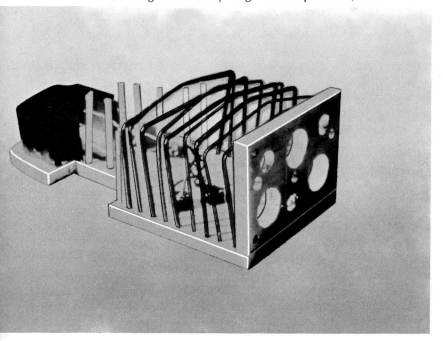

Reality and Probability

The area of probability is somewhat different. This time the event or situation is likely – it probably did or could in fact happen. Concern with reality is much closer and the observation more objective. Scale becomes important again and the forces of function in the utilitarian sense begin to operate.

A historical model of a medieval house or a Victorian bridge, for instance, will engage many children and will open up obvious opportunities for pupils to research and collect references.

Direct observation of real situations, such as a railway station, a pedestrian bridge, a dock or a cargo boat unloading, can be starting points not only for working models but for alternative suggestions. Observations of environmental and social subjects can lead to projects which postulate a new railway station, a different bridge, or another method of unloading cargo.

As well as moving in the world outside school and responding to the contemporary scene, situations can be set up within the immediate classroom/workshop, which take advantage of children's capacity to invent.

Photograph by Camera Press Ltd.

After observation a ten year-old identifies problems and possibilities.

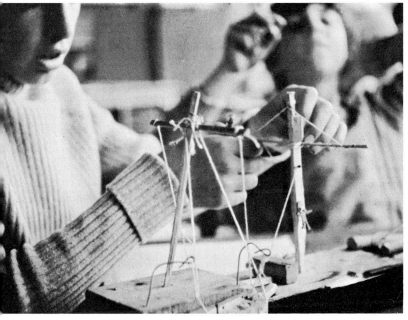

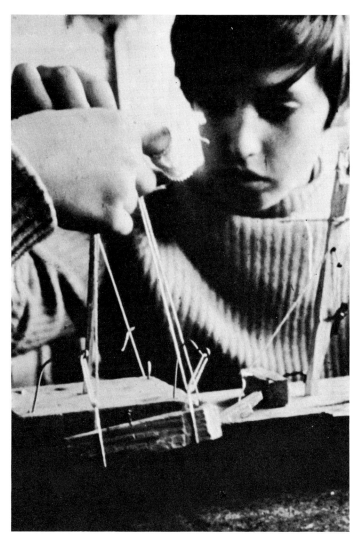

Two boys show their inventiveness.

The need is for problems and questions which intrigue and capture the imagination. The maze illustrated stemmed from a discussion on puzzles. The boys had worked on a maze for a table-tennis ball. Not being satisfied with their initial answer, which had to be hand-held, they moved on and invented a means whereby they could manipulate and control the image by pulling cords attached to it. It is interesting to note here that function intervened only in the sense that the construction had to operate for them. Their use of drawing pins, polythene and scrap material reveals their priorities and objectives.

The role of the teacher in this instance was subtle, giving help and guidance without demanding adult craft values. The children's inventiveness and obvious involvement in their work is proof enough of his effectiveness. At the same time, however, in the same school, another boy made a moving articulated toy, constructed with infinite care and precision from a series of handmade identical units, linked by pivots. The success of the boy's work depended on a precise attitude to measurement, to careful marking out and to accurate tool work. This time the teacher was not only able to promote the child's skill to the

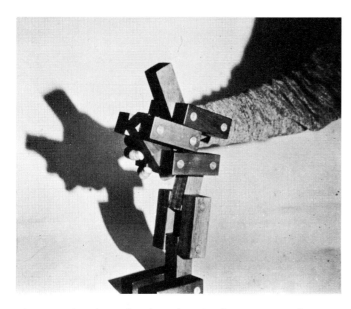

This articulated toy developed in this boy a sense of craftsmanship and a need for skill.

Reality and probability. Children's ideas for a baby rattle and a block of flats.

necessary level, but also brought the boy to realize the mechanics of his idea.

The area of probability is preoccupied not so much with fantasy as with extending, or adding to, reality. The starting point is real enough – whether it is a child's toy, an idea for a block of flats, or ways in which the human hand could be lengthened to pick apples off a tree – yet the ideas children formulate, extend and add to what we know. In their response to actual observation, children's work is seldom unrealistic; but the probability of their work is often missed by the adult who looks only for the answer he knows.

Problem and Concept

Perhaps the most easily discussed starting point is one where the teacher sets up a specific problem to resolve or introduces a new concept. In this way, the teacher can control and direct more precisely the experience children have. By giving the children a 'brief' at the outset, the teacher not only describes the problem and opportunities, but also contains the field of activity and concern that is open to the pupils at any one time.

To discuss this approach more fully, we have again defined two main areas:

(a) Problem-solving
(b) Basic design concepts.

Problem Solving

Along with the recent realization by many craft and handicraft teachers that their media should offer children more than a tool skill or a therapeutic alternative to the school desk, has come an awareness that by using materials in a problem-solving situation, a valuable contribution to a child's cognitive development can be made. Whereas many traditional craft exercises absolved children from real decision-making or involvement in the design of the exercise, the practice now is to expose children to the complete process of problem identification – the proposing of design alternatives, the resolving of production procedure, and finally, the making of an objective evaluation of their made-up prototype.

Clearly this move implies that more than tool skill is being looked for by the teacher. The opportunity for children to participate in the design of what they make, and the numerous decisions that follow, means that the teacher is now able to look for creative potential; to encourage the child's ability to analyze and to reason. It follows, therefore, that any final assessment of what children do under this heading, must accept values and acknowledge achievement other than simply that of craft expertise.

Perhaps the most critical stage in setting up a 'problem-solving' situation is, in fact, the beginning – 'the brief'. For the brief states, contains and limits the problem. The statement we make to children at the start, must be clear and precise, yet give them scope to think out the situation. We must be careful not to state the solution; for instance,

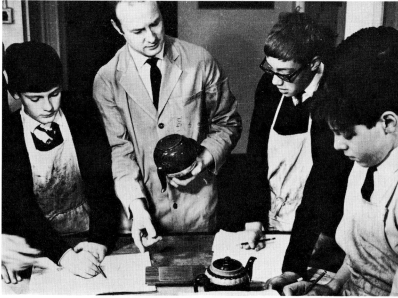

What exactly is the problem?

if we take a traditional handicraft exercise – the teapot stand – and introduce a brief such as

'Design and make a teapot stand',

we see that in fact the brief describes a solution to the *real problem*, which is one of insulation! It would be better if the brief were

'Devise and construct a means of preventing a hot teapot making marks on a polished wooden table'.

This time we have described the actual problem, and though in the event some children may arrive at a conventional teapot stand, others may find alternatives which we ourselves have not considered. We must be sure the brief allows the child room to think out the problem from first principles, rather than limiting his action to one of restyling or imitating a preconceived solution.

While it is important to keep the brief reasonably open-ended, so as to allow the child's imagination to operate, it may be advantageous on occasions deliberately to limit the materials or processes available.

'Using ⅛ in. thick acrylic sheet, design and produce a device to support four toothbrushes on the wall, above the handbasin in the bathroom'.

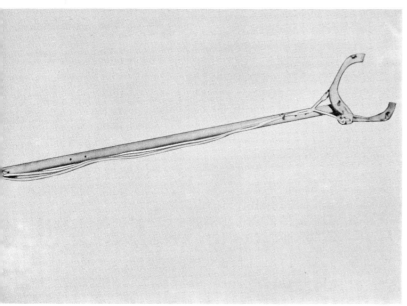
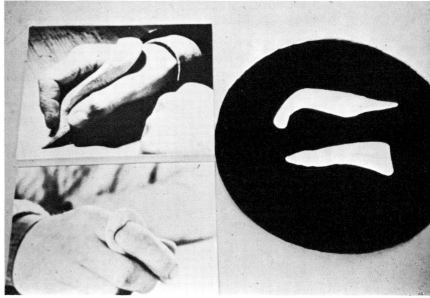

'Apple picker' and a 'biro' – children's ideas produced in response to specific problems.

This might be a convenient brief to follow up initial experimental work with Perspex. The brief then has the added intention of building on and taking advantage of previous experience and specific knowledge.

Just as children need help and guidance in order to gain their own skill in the handling of tools and materials, so, too, they need help in analyzing the given problem – suggestions on how to develop ideas, where to find information, advice on constructional detail, etc. The teacher should no more ignore his responsibilities in these instances than he would in the actual practical situation. In the 'problem-solving' situation, the teacher's role is as much concerned with helping children to think and resolve, as it is to produce and manufacture artifacts.

One of the most obvious ways a teacher can help children, is to 'set up' and *demonstrate* the problem; for instance, actually to put a 'hot teapot on a polished wooden surface' and let the children observe what happens. A problem that is *seen* or personally experienced is more likely to be understood.

Wherever possible, the actual environmental and social conditions that surround a problem, whether of an individual or a group, should be revealed and examined. Too often, although we may deal with real life problems, they are nevertheless considered in the abstract, and isolated from their real context.

Although there are plenty of 'problem-solving situations' in everyday life, other problems with no conventional utilitarian context can be set up.

'Design and produce a mechanical device to lift the given nut over a 3 in. wall and then deposit it in the given container'.

On the surface this problem might seem a useless exercise. Yet if we consider beyond the restricting influence of utilitarian function, we realize a purpose to the problem – to get children to think, to invent and, in this case, to apply certain principles of mechanics.

In another school, boys were given a standard model propeller and four plastic wheels, and then asked to 'construct a dragster that makes use of the propeller for its motive power'. Again, the problem and the brief were designed to extend the children's capacity for inventiveness and to allow certain academic knowledge to be utilized in a practical situation.

Though the context of a problem can stem from many different points, there are two overall questions that must be satisfied. Firstly, does the 'problem' encourage the child to use his imagination and his intellect? Secondly, does the 'problem' take into account the particular age, stage of development and personal interests of the child?

73

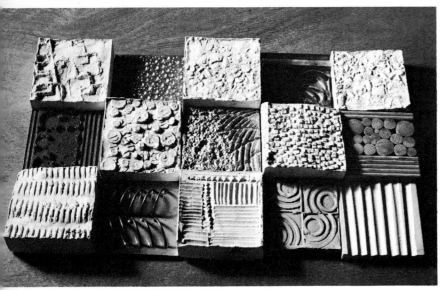

Finding textures and making a clay impression.

Observation of texture translated into plaster, metal and wood. Photograph by John Hunnex.

Basic Design Concepts

The moment children begin to use materials in a 3-dimensional context, they inevitably become involved with surface texture, pattern, the organization of form and shape in space, and colour and the effect of light. However, the involvement they have with these basic concepts is normally at an unconscious level – their immediate attention and concern being focused on 'making it work', 'putting it together', or simply being absorbed by their idea or image.

The advantage of starting from one of these concepts, be it pattern, texture, colour, space, shape, or whatever, is that one can present at a conscious level, what was always there, but seldom noticed. If we isolate these 'visual concepts' from actuality, they remain abstract and often meaningless to children. We need, therefore, to make every effort to relate these concepts back to the everyday situation.

For example, if we are using 'texture' as a starting point, we can accelerate a child's awareness of this simply by asking him to look around him, to touch and feel the material within his own immediate environment. A walk round the school taking rubbings, plasticine impressions and afterwards plaster moulds, will add new dimensions and a fresh awareness of his surroundings, a new understanding of materials and the surface textures peculiar to them. The stimulus of his own environment can sponsor a search to create new surfaces and textures.

The panel illustrated grew from a group attempt to devise individual texture blocks in wood and metal. Experience such as this could then be exploited in the surface decoration of a box, or in the making of blocks for fabric printing.

Children's perception of shape and form is often limited, and unless a conscious effort is made by the teacher to extend that awareness, their work may never move beyond a naïve schema. Again it is a matter of bringing the child to a new understanding of how shape and form can define and strengthen an idea. The example on page 75 shows attention being focused on shape through building 'silhouettes' (a natural extension of children's 2-dimensional drawing). From here, projects concerned with 'relief' and 'form' could grow.

Exploiting geometric arrangements is another natural way of extending a child's ability to handle shape. By systematic cutting, reorganizing, overlapping, and assembly, simple geometric units take on unforeseen form and stimulate new possibilities.

The danger of using 'basic design concepts' is that projects based on them can all too easily become little more than academic exercises that leave children untouched. They must certainly never be the total sum of a child's visual experience with materials. Instead, they can and should be a foundation for other possibilities; a reference area from which children draw confidence and stimulus for other ideas.

The starting points that have been discussed are, of course, only a handful of possible beginnings. Other

Looking at shape through silhouettes.

Geometry – paper to jewellery.

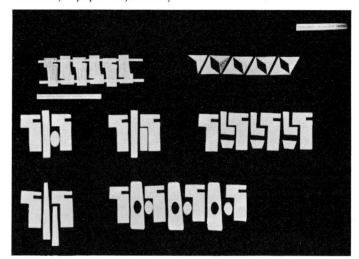

75

Constructional and mechanical exercises can be used to promote inventiveness.

teachers may prefer to start from a *theme* or a *topic* such as 'Flight', 'Transport', 'Communication', 'The Fairground', 'The Church', or 'The Community'; or again others might use a local situation, event or celebration as the initial focus.

At other times, phenomena such as 'Light', 'Speed', 'Sound', 'Gravity', could be used as starting points, as could looking at the potential of a car, electricity, the value of buoyancy or the use of wind. Some teachers will prefer to let children's work with materials stem from other aspects of the curriculum, from history, science, from environmental studies or from drama.

The only sure thing is that there are many starting points and as many possibilities in them as there are children – I have pinpointed just a few. There are also as many ways of using the same starting point as there are teachers. For this reason, I have not laid down any specific approach – for it is in a teacher's own presentation of whatever focus he uses, that the real value lies.

Academic exercises or a foundation for something else?

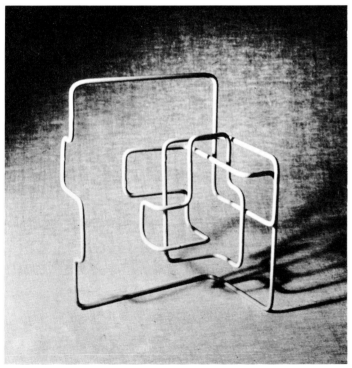

Chapter 6

Facilities

When the use of resistant materials is being discussed, whether in secondary, middle or primary schools, whether in the workshop, art room or classroom, before long questions about the provision of facilities and space, and the storage of tools and safety emerge. 'What tools are necessary?' 'How can I do anything in such a small space?' 'Isn't the equipment very expensive?' 'Where can I put all the materials and unfinished work?' These kind of questions are put by many, if not all, teachers at some point in their teaching.

Since the use of resistant materials was introduced into the curriculum, considerable experience has been gained in the provision of the necessary facilities and accommodation. Unfortunately many of the expectations and assumptions often made today about the number of tools needed, about the equipment and its location, stem not so much from what *is* needed, as from what *was* necessary. For instance, the traditional handicraft premise that each boy needs a separate kit of tools and a separate bench, is perhaps logical in a course where all the boys are doing the same thing at the same time – but is it necessary for the work and activities we discussed earlier?

Tools and Equipment

Today, as a result of the development of the 'Do-It-Yourself' market, many of the traditional specialist tools are being replaced by more general purpose equipment, and many previously time-consuming operations, some of which demanded considerable skill, are being carried out by small machine tools. New adhesives and constructional techniques are making some tools obsolete.

The provision of tools and equipment must be related to the materials you intend to introduce. They should acknowledge the type of work being attempted, and be sufficient for the number of children engaged at any one time.

The list of tools and equipment on pages 79–80 assumes that a range of materials will be used, i.e. wood, metal, plastic and concrete, that the work undertaken will be individual rather than prescriptive, and that a maximum of twenty children would be using the facilities at the same time.

The list is divided into three categories and aims at distinguishing between what is absolutely essential to begin with and what may become necessary and useful as the work develops. Clearly there can be no definitive list. Each teacher and each school will have their own priorities, and while some of the tools and equipment listed may be unnecessary, others may be essential to a teacher's particular way of working.

It is wise to start in a modest way, with a minimum of tools and equipment, then slowly build up resources according to individual needs. In the past, some teachers have allowed their teaching to become suffocated by an over-zealous collection of tools. This often led to a series of 'exercises' which were little more than a tedious journey through a catalogue of tools and processes. Tools should be used as a means to an end, rather than their use becoming an end in itself.

Which tools are really necessary?

In this middle school most tools are kept on a trolley.

TOOLS		CONSUMABLES	EQUIPMENT & MACHINERY
A basic kit to get going	5 8″ fine-tooth tenon saws 1 10″ tenon saw 1 cross-cut hand saw 2 junior hacksaws plus spare blades 2 standard hacksaws plus spare blades 1 doz. mixed surform tools plus spare blades 6 handfiles 2nd cut: 2 flat, 2 half round, 2 round 3 cork sanding blocks 4 hammers: 2 12-oz., 2 4-oz. 2 pincers 3 pairs of pliers	*Supply of:* Glasspaper Fine emery cloth Cellulose lacquer Paints, turps *Selection of:* Nails, screws and small bolts *Supply of:* P.V.A. glue	Heavy benches or bench space fitted with vices, 6 wood type and 3 metal 2 Stanley table vices 5 bench hooks Hot wire cutter Strip heater (for plastics)

	TOOLS	CONSUMABLES	EQUIPMENT & MACHINERY
A basic kit to get going (cont.)	2 pairs of tin snips: 1 flat, 1 curved 1 set of firmer chisels, 1" to ¼" 2 mallets 1 brace and set of bits, 1" to ⅜" 2 hand-drills and set of drills, ¼" to ⅛" 1 countersunk bit 1 smoothing plane 3 4" screwdrivers 2 bradawls 6 metal rules, e.g. 5 12", 1 3' 3 engineers' 4" squares 2 plastic washing-up bowls 2 small garden trowels 10 G. clamps: 2 6", 6 4", 2 2" 2 electric soldering irons: 1 25 watt, 1 65 watt 1 medium/fine oilstone	Evostick Tensol B cement Core solder '3-in-one' oil ½" paint brushes String, elastic bands Balsa cement	
Will become necessary	2 coping saws plus spare blades 4 2' 6" sash cramps 2 pairs of round nosed pliers 1 nail punch 1 centre punch 1 ⅝" shoulder plane 1 set of spanners 1 12" Try square 1 mole wrench 1 staple gun 1 6" screwdriver 1 hand 'Pop Riveter' and supply of rivets 1 'Marples' mitre saw 1 disc cutter to fit hand-drill	More detailed range of fittings and fixtures, ie. hinges Perspex polish 'Cascamite' powder Petrobond casting sand	Bench shears Pillar drill Jig saw Brazing hearth and torch Lathe for metal Two-way compressor Small kiln
Could be useful at some time	1 set of gouges (not too fine) 1 'Abrofile' 1 set of needle files 2 spokeshaves: 1 flat, 1 curved 1 hand router 1 hand vice 1 rip saw 1 pair of dividers 2 gauges: 1 marking, 1 cutting 2 jack planes Extra files, chisels and planes 1 glass cutter		Sanding disc (Bench model) Lathe for wood Portable flexible drive drill Grinderette Vacuum bag

Forelands Middle School, Isle of Wight. A general view showing the art and craft area.

Space and layout

Although the use of various materials has been discussed, the philosophy that separates and isolates the working of these different materials has never been advanced or accepted. Instead, we have suggested arguments for the grouping of materials under the general term 'resistant materials'. It follows, therefore, that in planning a working area we should envisage these materials coming under one roof. Although from time to time individual materials will require special facilities and even different working conditions, this in itself should not lead to arrangements which isolate and segregate the working of one material from another. The opportunity to work in an environment where ideas can move and grow from one material to another, where different materials can join together in one idea, is essential in the early stages. It is a necessary prerequisite of a child's understanding of the potential of working with materials and of his appreciation of the possibilities of his own ideas. The thoughts and layouts that have been discussed and illustrated therefore assume a basic premise: *that the necessary resources that relate to working with 'resistant materials' should be easily available and kept in close proximity.* This understood, we then have to plan our work area with regard to layout, the organization of resources and the safeguarding of proper safety precautions.

Rather than argue about the square footage required to accommodate twenty children working with materials, let us consider some of the essential services and accommodation that will be required and then see how these might be fitted together. We shall need:

Planning and Reference Area: a place where the children can plan and draw out ideas – test them by simple paper, card or balsa wood models, etc. Where they can refer to books and magazines for information. A place that can accommodate a display area as well as 'stimulus' and 'resource' material, be it a bird's skull, driftwood, a carburettor, a slide projector or a magnifying glass.

General Construction Area: a place where the assembly and the larger part of the actual manipulation of the material takes place. Essential here will be the provision of sturdy work surfaces and ample holding devices, such as vices. This area needs to be, in part at least, highly flexible; the accommodation of various activities and the working of different materials, and the provision of different 'working tops' that can fit and interchange with the standard bench will do much to achieve this flexibility.

Specific Technique/Process Areas: these areas will become necessary as the range and level of work de-

velops. Three areas at least should be planned early on.

Heat Area – a well protected area, ventilated and, if possible, with a stone floor and a sand pit for metal casting. Should accommodate a brick hearth and gas services (much can be done with bottled gas). A kiln and plenty of sockets for soldering and plastics-forming equipment.

Dirty Area – ideally with a tiled floor and drain so that the area can be washed down. This would become the area for clay, plaster, concrete, painting etc. Requests for a double sink (one with 'box' drain) should be made.

Machine Area – even if no machine tools are envisaged at first, plan an area with good supply of sockets and a cut out system. The extent of the area will depend on the work being undertaken and the capitation allowance.

Storage Areas: perhaps one of the main reasons why many teachers avoid using a range of 'resistant materials' is that they are so short of storage space. While some floor space is essential within the general work area, with a little imagination much more use could be made of space under benches, overhead, outside. Many schools seem to give more room to hats and coats than to materials, and early contact with planners should ensure that the case for storage is put very forcibly. About equal amounts of area will be needed for storing materials and for work in progress.

Heat area.

Storage area showing access through to the area for clay and plaster.

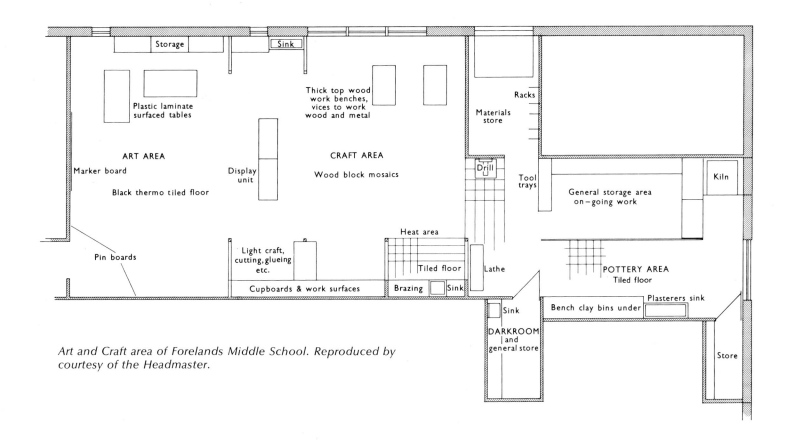

Art and Craft area of Forelands Middle School. Reproduced by courtesy of the Headmaster.

A theoretical layout showing a suggested breakdown of a given area.

Storage Materials	Reference area Planning, Drawing, Reading and Seeking Information, Display, Library and Museum		Storage Work in Progress
	Construction Area Flexible bench/work surface system. To accommodate up to 10 children at benches with vices – and up to 6 places at plain work surfaces.		
Heat Area	Machine Tool Area	Dirty Area	

Index

acrylic 42
adhesives, synthetic 51
alienation of man from materials 16, *17*
aluminium alloys 41

balsa wood 40
Bauhaus 17, *17*
'Bilofix' 42
brass wire 4
bricks 35, *38*, 42
briefs 72–3

chalk 42
construction
    basic impulses of 7, 9
    the purpose and problem of 46, 48,
        48, *49*, *50*
concrete 35, *39*
construction kits, commercially
    available 33, *33*, *34*, 41, 42, 53, *53*

design concepts 74–6
designs
    children's 43
    development and realization of 54–6
dowelling jigs 51, *51*
drawing *see* sketching and drawing
driftwood 40

'Durox' 42

education, responsibility of 16
electrical/electronic components 35,
    37, 42
equipment 78–80
exercises, constructional and
    mechanical *76*, *77*

fencing staves 40
forms, perception of 74

galvanized wire 41
geometrical arrangements 74–5, *75*
gilding metal wire 41
granules, expanded polystyrene 42
Gropius, Walter 17

handicrafts, traditional concept of 9,
    16, 17, 24–5, 43
hardwood 40

ideas
    stimuli for 66–71
    translating into physical form 18, 21,
        22, 24, 54–6, 72–3
imagination, children's 66–71
insulation blocks 35, 42
iron, soft 41
iron wire, soft *28*, *29*, *30*

jigs 1, *51*, 52

'Kayem' 41

'Lego' 33, 42

machine tools 35, *37*, 79–80
mahogany wood 40
materials
    as a source of inspiration 59
    for different age groups 24, 27, *28*,
        29, *29*, 30, 35, *35*
    physical qualities of 74–6
    range of 27
    realizing the physical potential of
        59, *60*, *61*, 62–4
    role of in society 7
    sources of 30, 33, 35, 40–2, 58–9, *59*,
        60
    studying the qualities of 62–4
materials, building 35, *38*, *39*, 42
'Meccano' 33, *34*, 41, 42, 53, *53*
mercanti wood 40
metal *28*, *29*, *31*, 41
model making 56, *57*

obeche wood 40

'Petrobond' casting sand 41
pillar drills 51, *51*
plastics 7, 42
play, importance of 18–21
plywood 40, *64*, *65*
polystyrene, expanded 42
polythene sheeting 42
pop riveters 51, *51*
problem-solving 72–3, *73*
PVC, rigid 42

resources *see* materials
'Richard's house' 18–21, *19*, *20*, 68

sand 41, 42
sandstone 42
scrap materials 30, *30*, *31*, 59, *60*
shapes, perception of 74–5, *75*
'Siporex' 42
sketching and drawing 55–6, *56*, *57*, 68
softwood 40
soldering 41
spot welders 51
steel sheeting 41
steel tube 41
stone 42

textures, perception of 74, *74*
thermoplastic 42
tin plate 41
tools 51, 78–80
    use of by children 24–6
    see also machine tools
tool-skills, teaching of 25–6, 43, *44*, *45*

veneers 40
'Vinamold' wax 42

wax 42
welding rods 41
wire
    galvanized 41
    gilding metal 41
wire cutters *28*
wood 40, *64*, *65*
work areas
    arrangement of 81–3
    Forelands Middle School 83
    Gloucestershire comprehensive
        school 23, *23*
    Isle of Wight middle school 22

zinc alloy 41